CHART HITS OF '02-'03

ISBN 0-634-05676-X

HAL•LEONARD
CORPORATION
7777 W. BLUEMOUND RD. P.O. BOX 13819 MILWAUKEE, WI 5321

Visit Hal Leonard Online at
www.halleonard.com

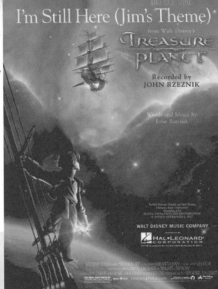

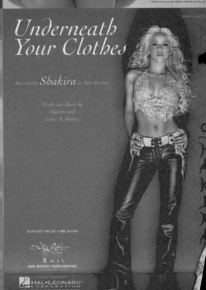

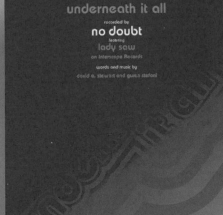

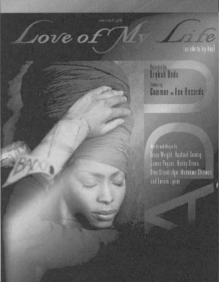

BEAUTIFUL

Words and Music by
LINDA PERRY

Moderately slow

Whispered: Don't look at me.

Ev-'ry-day ___ is so
To all your friends ___ you're de-

DILEMMA

Words and Music by CORNELL HAYNES,
ANTWON MAKER, KENNETH GAMBLE
and BUNNY SIGLER

Slow Groove

BRING ON THE RAIN

Words and Music by BILLY MONTANA
and HELEN DARLING

COMPLICATED

Words and Music by AVRIL LAVIGNE, LAUREN CHRISTY,
SCOTT SPOCK and GRAHAM EDWARDS

Moderate Pop

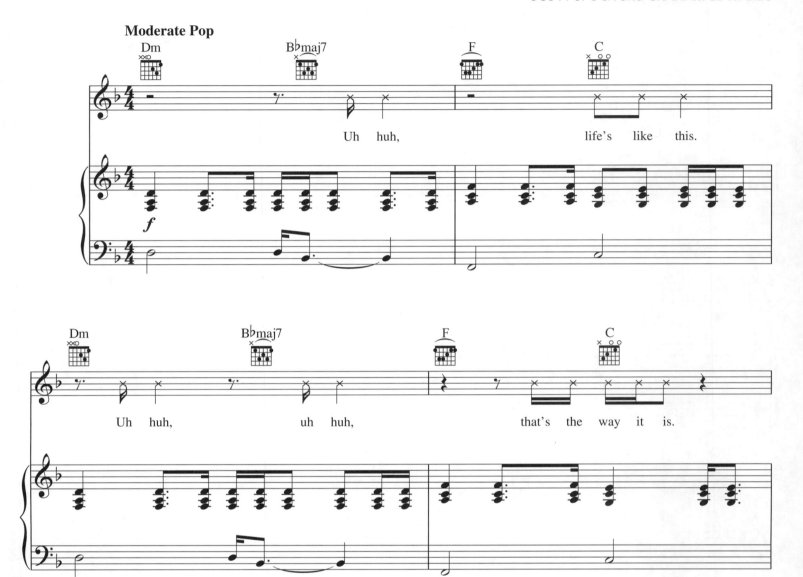

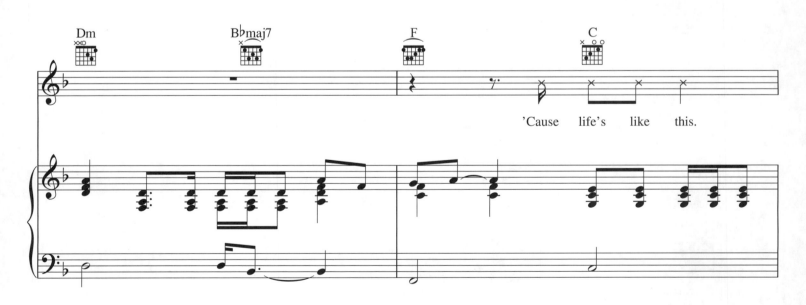

CRY

Words and Music by
ANGIE APARO

D.S. al Coda

DISEASE

Words and Music by ROB THOMAS
and MICK JAGGER

Original key: A♭ minor. This edition has been transposed up one half-step to be more playable.

FOOLISH

Words and Music by IRVING LORENZO
and A. DOUGLAS

Whispered: Mur-der Inc.

A - shan - ti.

See my days are cold __ with-out you but I'm hurt-in' while __ I'm with

DON'T KNOW WHY

Words and Music by
JESSE HARRIS

DON'T MESS WITH MY MAN

Words and Music by BRANDON D. CASEY,
BRIAN D. CASEY and BRYAN MICHAEL COX

THE GAME OF LOVE

Words and Music by RICK NOWELS
and GREGG ALEXANDER

(Guitar Solo ad lib.)

(Make ___ me feel good, yeah.)

HEAVEN

Words and Music by BRYAN ADAMS
and JIM VALLANCE

Moderate Dance beat

Ba - by you're all ___ that I want when you're

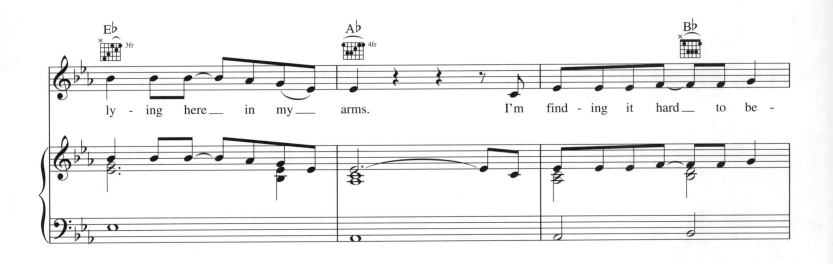

ly - ing here ___ in my ___ arms. I'm find - ing it hard ___ to be -

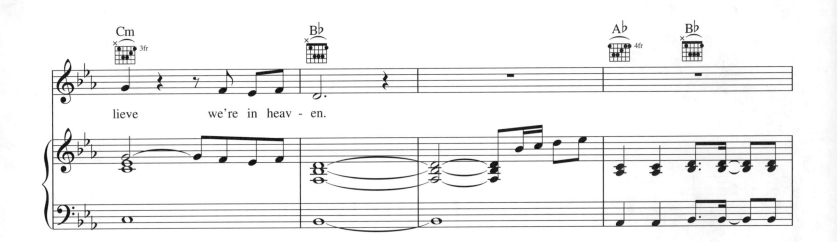

lieve we're in heav - en.

Spoken: We're in heav-en.

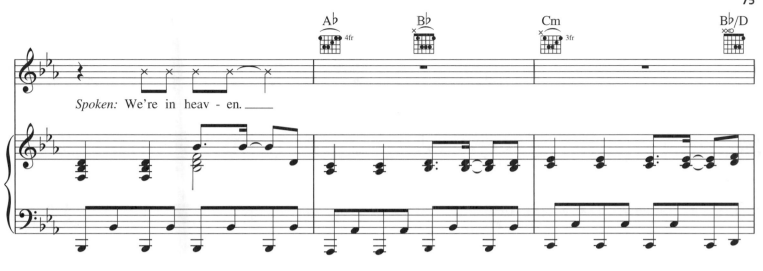

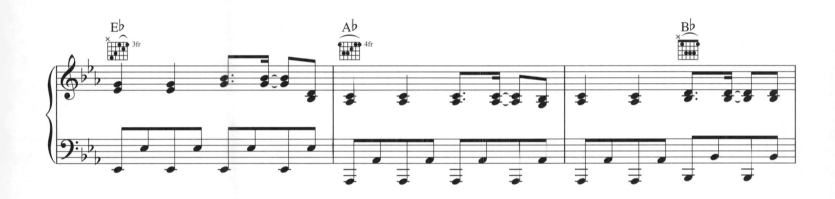

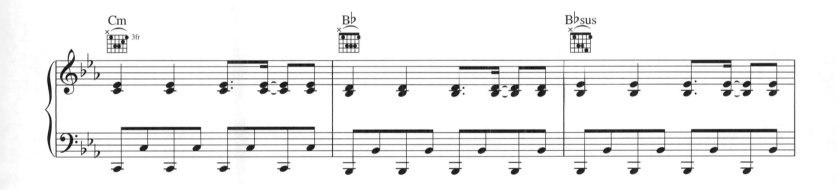

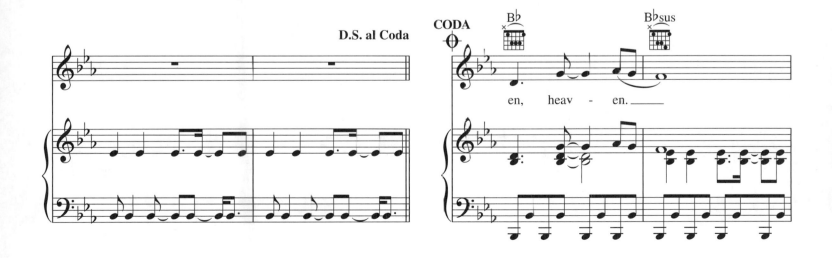

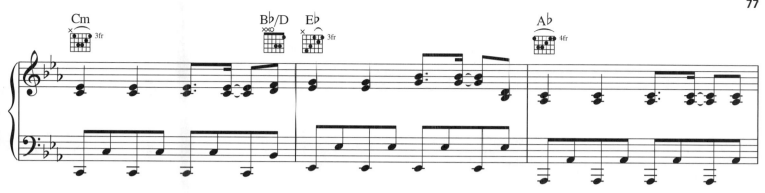

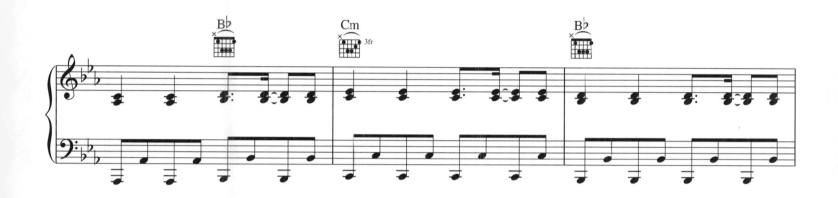

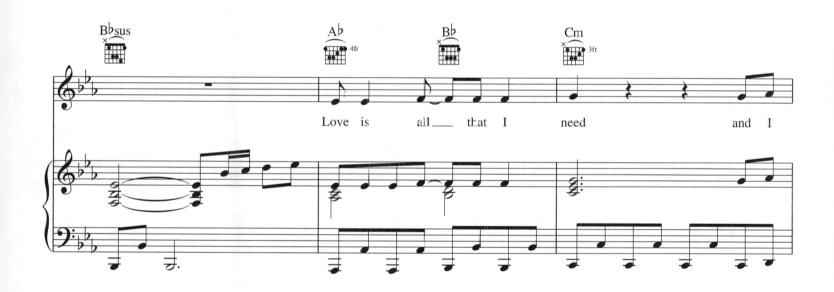

Love is all___ that I need and I

found it there___ in your heart. It

I'M WITH YOU

Words and Music by AVRIL LAVIGNE, LAUREN CHRISTY,
SCOTT SPOCK and GRAHAM EDWARDS

I'M STILL HERE
(Jim's Theme)
from Walt Disney's TREASURE PLANET

Words and Music by
JOHN RZEZNIK

JENNY FROM THE BLOCK

Words and Music by TROY OLIVER, ANDRE DEYO,
JENNIFER LOPEZ, JEAN CLAUDE OLIVIER,
SAMUEL BARNES, JOSE FERNANDO ARBEX MIRO,
LAWRENCE PARKER, SCOTT STERLING and M. OLIVER

Moderate Hip Hop

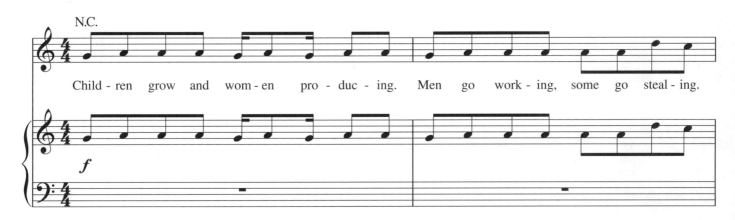

Chil-dren grow and wom-en pro-duc-ing. Men go work-ing, some go steal-ing.

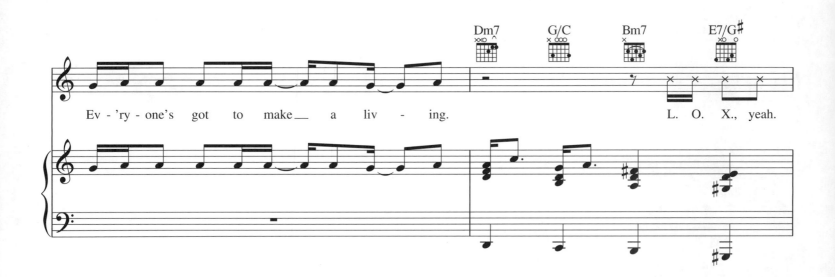

Ev-'ry-one's got to make a liv-ing. L. O. X., yeah.

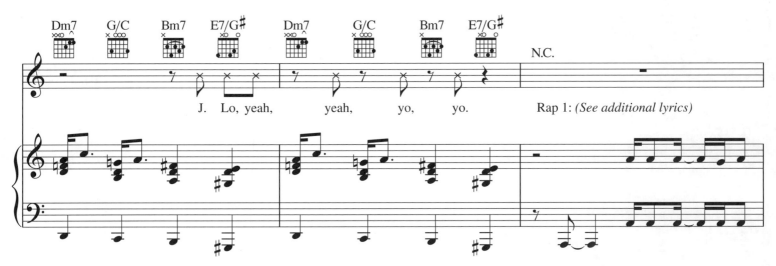

J. Lo, yeah, yeah, yo, yo. Rap 1: *(See additional lyrics)*

lit-tle, now I have a-lot. No mat-ter where I go I know where I came from, _ from the Bronx. Don't be

fooled by the rocks that I got. I'm still, I'm still Jen-ny from the block. Used to have a

lit-tle, now I have a-lot. No mat-ter where I go I know where I came from, _ from the Bronx.

Additional Lyrics

Rap 1:   We off the blocks this year.
Went from a 'lil to a lot this year.
Everybody mad at the rocks that I wear.
I know where I'm goin' and I know where I'm from.
You hear LOX in the air.
Yeah we at the airport out.
D-block from the block where everybody air forced out.
Wit' a new white tee you fresh. Nothin' phony wit' us.
Make the money, get the mansion, bring the homies wit' us.

Rap 2:   Yo, it take hard work to cash checks
So don't be fooled by the rocks that I got, they're assets.
You get back what you put out.
Even if you take the good route, can't count the hood out.
After a while you'll know who to blend wit'.
Just keep it real wit' the ones you came in wit'.
Best thing to do is stay low, LOX and J. Lo.
They act like they don't, but they know.

JUST LIKE A PILL

Words and Music by ALECIA MOORE
and DALLAS AUSTIN

LANDSLIDE

Words and Music by
STEVIE NICKS

LOVE OF MY LIFE
(An Ode to Hip Hop)

Words and Music by ERICA WRIGHT, RAPHAEL SAADIQ,
JAMES POYSER, BOBBY OZUNA, GLEN STANDRIDGE,
MADUKWU CHINWAH and LONNIE LYNN

Spoken: *Right here what we gon' do is go back.* Way back.

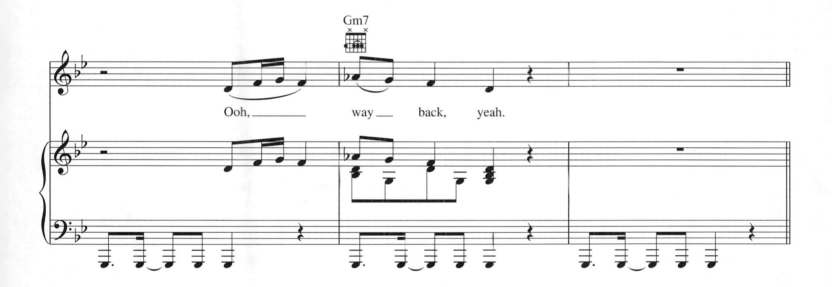

Ooh, _____ way _ back, yeah.

I met him when I was a, a lit-tle girl. He gave, he gave me po-et-ry and

freak. How could it be that it was all just so sim-ple then? A teen-age love but you say,

Additional Lyrics

Rap: Ya'll know how I met her.
We broke up and got back together.
To get her back I had to sweat her.
Thought she'd roll with bad boys forever.
In many ways them boys may be better.
To grow, I had to let her.
She needed cheddar and I understood that.
Lookin' for cheese, that don't make her a hood rat.
In fact, she's a queen to me.
Her light beams on me.
I love it when she sings to me.
It's like that now.

LIKE I LOVE YOU

Words and Music by PHARRELL WILLIAMS,
CHAD HUGO and JUSTIN TIMBERLAKE

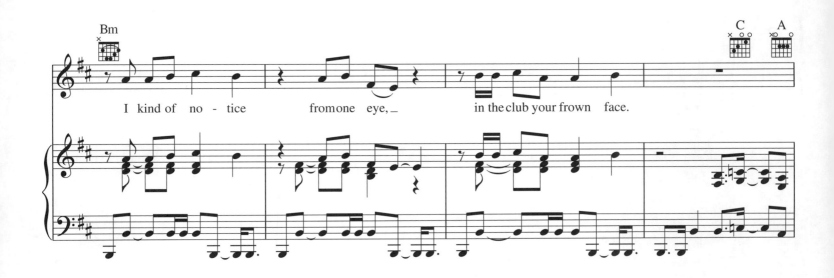

Additional Lyrics

Rap 1: Just somethin' about you.
Way I'm lookin' at you, whatever.
Keep lookin' at me.
Gettin' scared now, right?
Don't fail me baby, it's just Justin.
Feel good right, listen

Rap 2: Ma, what's you wanna do?
I'm in front of you.
Grab a friend, see I can have fun with two.
Or me and you put on a stage show
In the mall kids, that's how to change low.
Point to her, they say, "Wow it's the same glow."
Point to me, I say, "Yeah, it's the same dough."
We the same type. You my air of life.
You have me sleepin' in the same bed ev'ry night.

Go ride with me, you deservin' the best.
Take a few shots, let it burn in your chest.
We could ride 'em down pumpin' N.E.R.D. in the deck.
Funny how a few words turned into sex.
Play number 3, joint called "brain."
Ma took a hit, made me swerve in the lane.
The name Malicious and I burn every track.
Clipse and J. Timberlake, now how heavy is that?

Rap 3: You know, I used to dream about this when I was a little boy.
I never thought it would end up this way, drums.
It's kind of special right? Yeah.
You know you think about it.
Sometimes people just destined. Destined to do what they do.
And that's what it is.
Now everybody dance.

A MOMENT LIKE THIS

Words and Music by JOHN REID
and JORGEN KJELL ELOFSSON

Original key: C♯ minor. This edition has been transposed up one half-step to be more playable.

Some peo-ple search___ for-ev-er for that one spe-cial kiss.___

Oh, I can't be-lieve___ it's hap - pen-ing___ to me._____ Some

peo-ple wait___ a life - time for a mo - ment___ like this.___

Choir: (Mo-ment like this.)___
Lead vocal ad lib.

A NEW DAY HAS COME

Words and Music by STEPHAN MOCCIO
and ALDO NOVA

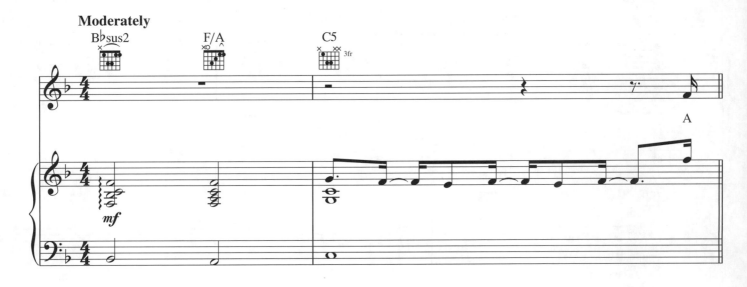

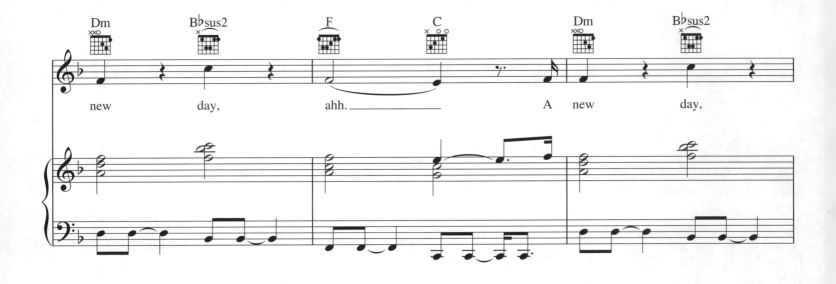

Original key: F♯ major. This edition has been transposed down one half-step to be more playable.

SK8ER BOI

Words and Music by AVRIL LAVIGNE, LAUREN CHRISTY,
SCOTT SPOCK and GRAHAM EDWARDS

Lively Rock

He was a boy. She was a girl.

Can I make it an - y more ob - vi - ous? He was a punk.

She did bal - let. What more can I say?

SOAK UP THE SUN

Words and Music by JEFF TROTT
and SHERYL CROW

SOMEWHERE OUT THERE

Words and Music by RAINE MAIDA,
JEREMY TAGGART and DUNCAN COUTTS

Last time I talked to you, you were lone-ly and out of place.
Down here in the at-mos-phere, gar-bage and cit-y lights.

You were look-in' down on me, lost out in space.
You've gone to save your tired soul. You've gone to save our lives.

Original key: D♭ major. This edition has been transposed up one half-step to be more playable.

UNDERNEATH YOUR CLOTHES

Words and Music by SHAKIRA
and LESTER A. MENDEZ

You're a song __ writ-ten by the hands of God. __
'Cause of you, __ I for-got the smart ways to lie. __

__ Don't get me wrong __ 'cause this might sound to you a bit odd. __ But you own the place __
__ Be-cause of you __ I'm run-ning out of rea-sons to cry. __ When the friends are gone, __

__ where all my thoughts go hid - ing. Right un-der your clothes __ is
__ when the par-ty's o - ver, we will still be-long __

UNDERNEATH IT ALL

Words and Music by DAVID A. STEWART
and GWEN STEFANI

Moderate Reggae

It's times when I want some-one more,___ a-some-one more like me,___

and there's times when this_ dress re-hear-sal seems in-com-plete,___ but

real, 'cause un - der - neath it all, you are my real Prince Charm - ing. Like the

8vb throughout

heat from the fi - re you were al - ways burn - ing. An - y - time you're a - round my bod - y keeps call - ing for your

touch, your kiss - es and your sweet ro - man - cing. There's an - oth - er side of you a - dis a - wo - man here a - dore. A -

side from your tem - per ev - 'ry - thing else se - cure. You - 're good for me, ba - by; of that I'm sure, 'cause

(8vb cont'd)

8vb to end

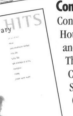